HEALTHY·LIVING·

Talking About

What You Eat

**By Hazel Edwards
and Goldie Alexander**

Gareth Stevens
Publishing

Please visit our Web site **www.garethstevens.com**. For a free color catalog of all our high-quality books, call toll free 1-800-542-2595 or fax 1-877-542-2596.

Library of Congress Cataloging-in-Publication Data

Edwards, Hazel.

 Talking about what you eat / Hazel Edwards and Goldie Alexander.

     p. cm. -- (Healthy living)

 Includes index.

 ISBN 978-1-4339-3656-2 (lib. bdg.)

 1. Nutrition--Juvenile literature. 2. Diet--Juvenile literature. I. Alexander, Goldie. II. Title.

 RA784.E324 2010

 613.2--dc22

                              2009043453

Published in 2010 by

Gareth Stevens Publishing

111 East 14th Street, Suite 349

New York, NY 10003

© 2010 Blake Publishing

For Gareth Stevens Publishing:

Art Direction: Haley Harasymiw

Editorial Direction: Kerri O'Donnell

Cover photo: iStockphoto.

Photos and illustrations:

Page 6 (food plate); iStockphoto, pages 4–5, 10–11, 13–23, 26–27, 30; Shutterstock.com, page 4 (bottom); MyPyramid.gov, page 7 (food pyramid); UC Publishing, pages 8 (bottom), 9 (top), 10 (bottom right), 12–13, 20–21, 23, 25–29.

Printed in the United States of America

CPSIA compliance information: Batch #CW10GS: For further information contact Gareth Stevens, New York, New York, at 1-800-542-2595.

Contents

What is food quality?

quality food diet **+** sensible eating habits **+** physical activity **=** healthy life

Have you heard the saying "You are what you eat"? It doesn't mean you're a cheese sandwich or a banana. It means that what you choose to eat has a huge effect on your general health and happiness.

Food quality is the value your body gets out of food. Making good food choices and having an active life will help you be the healthiest you can. It's important to develop good eating habits early in life.

Sometimes we develop poor eating habits. Why?

Some reasons for unhealthy food choices might be:

- being influenced by advertising
- feeling too tired to eat
- following someone else's choices
- not understanding enough about food

What do you need?

Here is a quick look at the types of food your body needs.

Protein: important for growth. Protein helps to build and repair body organs, skin, blood—even hair. Foods such as meat, fish, soybeans, milk, and cheese are excellent sources of protein.

Fats: concentrated and rich sources of **energy**.

Polyunsaturated fats: these include Omega-3 and Omega-6, essential fatty acids found in fish, vegetable, and nut oils. These are good for you.

Saturated fats: found in foods such as butter and meat fat. You need much less of these.

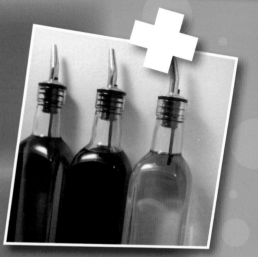

Carbohydrates: important for energy. Complex carbohydrates are found in vegetables and whole grains. Simple carbohydrates are found in sugary foods and provide less nutritional value. Eat more complex carbohydrates and less simple carbohydrates.

Water: essential! More than half of your body is water. Without it, your body cannot do all the jobs it needs to do to keep you alive. You lose some water just by breathing and much more by sweating. Drink water every day.

Vitamins and minerals: needed for proper growth and health. They are found in all good-quality foods. Eat these every day.

What should I choose?

The word **"nutrition"** describes all that you eat and drink. Good nutrition means having all the foods that your body needs in your daily meals. To help you do this, you can use the food pyramid.

Food is sorted into groups. You need to choose something from each group every day. But that doesn't mean you should have one strawberry, one carrot, one slice of bread, one egg, and then eat cheese for the rest of the day! The food pyramid helps you to understand which foods you should eat most often.

The pyramid is divided into sections of different sizes. These show you which foods you need to eat more of and which you should choose in smaller amounts.

What about all the other foods?

Some foods do not fit into the main food groups. They are not essential to provide the **nutrients** your body needs. Some contain too much added fat, salt, and sugar.

These extra foods, in small amounts, can add to the enjoyment of a healthy diet and can be chosen sometimes.

MyPyramid
STEPS TO A HEALTHIER YOU
MyPyramid.gov

| GRAINS | VEGETABLES | FRUITS | MILK | MEAT & BEANS |

Drink plenty of water

Calories count

What are calories?

Calories (cal) are units that measure the energy value of food. They allow us to talk about how much energy a food contains.

Carbohydrate = 4 cal per gram

Fat = 9 cal per gram

Calories tell us how much energy is burned up during exercise and other everyday activities.

1 apple: 65 cal

1 chocolate bar: 200 cal

We eat food to fuel our bodies for energy, growth, and repair.

The amount of carbohydrates, protein, and fat in a food adds up to its calorie content.

Young children and teenagers need lots of energy to fuel their growth and development.

The amount of energy we use varies from one person to the next. It depends on the build, gender, age, environment, and amount of physical activity the person does.

You use up more calories in a cold place than you would in the tropics. Why do you think this might happen?

Boiled egg: 69 cal
Fried egg: 100 cal
Sushi roll (large size): 136 cal

Energy to burn

In the past, families dug their own vegetable gardens, walked to the store and carried home the groceries, and chopped wood for the fire and stove. Today, we have cars, washing machines, supermarkets, and central heating. We don't burn off as many calories in our everyday lives as people did in the past.

We have more foods available to us today, including lots of ready-made foods. Many of these foods are high in energy—they have lots of calories—yet our lives are less active. If we eat more calories but use up fewer through physical activity, we gain weight and our health can suffer.

Our bodies store excess energy inside fat cells. It takes around 3,500 calories of energy to burn off one pound of body fat.

Physical activity:

- makes you feel fit, strong, and healthy
- releases chemicals called endorphins in your brain—these make you feel good
- keeps you from feeling stressed
- keeps your weight down
- strengthens your muscles
- helps you sleep better
- strengthens your heart and lungs
- strengthens your bones
- helps you look great

No physical activity:

- makes you feel sluggish
- slows down your brain
- can make you feel stressed
- helps you gain weight
- can make you sleep poorly
- keeps your heart and lungs from growing strong
- keeps your bones from becoming strong
- prevents you from looking as good as you can

How much energy?

Your body uses energy to keep it working properly. Extra energy is required for all your activities.

- Running uses twice as many calories as brisk walking.

- Walking up stairs uses about 60 times more calories than taking an elevator.

- Swimming laps uses at least 15 times more calories than standing to watch someone else swim.

- Playing ball uses around 60 times more calories than playing a computer game.

Compare the calorie content in these foods:

1 glass of cola = 110 cal

1 cup pineapple juice = 127 cal

1 cup strawberries = 30 cal

1 scoop vanilla ice cream = 90 cal

You don't have to be a world-class athlete to exercise. You can have fun:

- playing tag
- skipping
- using a hula hoop
- skateboarding
- riding a scooter
- in-line skating
- throwing a Frisbee
- playing wall ball
- flying a kite
- creating an aerobics routine

To burn off the calories from a small serving of french fries, someone who weighs 88 pounds would have to:

- sit for 16 hours
- walk for 2 hours
- run for 50 minutes

HOW FRESH ARE YOUR FRUITS AND VEGETABLES?

Is fresh always best?

You find words like "fresh" and "natural" in advertisements for food all the time. These words are used to grab your attention and make you believe that the product being sold is healthy. After all, who'd buy food advertised as stale or full of chemicals? But beware! Just because the sign says "fresh fruits and vegetables" does not mean that they are the best choice.

Did you know that the vitamin and mineral content of frozen or canned fruits and vegetables is sometimes higher than in the same things bought fresh? For example, green vegetables begin to lose vitamin C as soon as they are picked. If they are frozen right away, the vitamin C level is still high. Fresh vegetables usually go from the farm to a **wholesale** market before they get to the places where you shop. They may not make it into your cooking pot until two weeks after they were picked. By then, the vitamin C levels have dropped.

Understanding what happens to food before it reaches you can help you make decisions about what to buy.

How does your food get to you?

wholesale market

factory

farm

12

How has food quality changed?

In the past, you could only be sure of food quality if you grew your own fruits and vegetables. Food could be transported in open trucks, becoming dirty and polluted. All sorts of chemicals could be sprayed on food to stop insects from eating it. There were no strict rules for handling food. People could not buy anything that wasn't in season, because fruits and vegetables could not be stored for any length of time. As a result, there was less fresh fruit in winter.

Remember, not all the food sold in a country is grown there. It can come from any overseas country, where the food handling laws may be very different.

Laws protect your food quality

Today, every step of food processing—from the farm to the shopper—is carefully checked and covered by laws. These laws protect you. You can be sure of the quality of fruits and vegetables grown and processed here.

transportation

you, the shopper

supermarket

SUPERMARKET

FOOD SAFETY

When buying food, check to make sure that:

- the seal is unbroken
- the use-by date is displayed on the container
- the contents are not past their use-by date
- you can read the ingredients in your language

Keep your lunch cool!

SOS! For food safety: CHILL!

Wash fruits and vegetables before eating and/or cooking.

Put food that needs to be chilled in the fridge right away.

Foods that need to stay especially cold in your school lunch include:

- sandwiches or salads made with meat or chicken
- tuna and eggs
- milk, cheese, and yogurt

14

Keeping food safe

Have you ever gotten sick or had a stomachache and thought you had the flu? It might have been a **food-borne illness**. This means you got sick from eating spoiled food. Some people call this food poisoning.

Food can make you sick if it is spoiled by **bacteria** or mold. It may look, smell, and taste okay, but it can still make you sick.

Bacteria and mold need food, water, and a mild temperature in which to grow.

Bacteria thrive in foods rich in protein and water, such as eggs, meat, fish, poultry, and milk and other dairy products.

One way you can keep yourself from getting sick and keep bacteria from spreading is by washing your hands after going to the bathroom. You must also wash your hands before preparing or eating food.

The best way to wash your hands:

1. Wet your hands with warm water.

2. Put soap on your hands.

3. Wash your hands by rubbing them together for at least 20 seconds.

4. Rinse well with warm water.

5. Dry your hands with a clean towel or paper towel. Don't use your dish towel!

Keep raw food separate from other food.

Clean kitchen counters and equipment before you prepare food and after they have been used with raw food.

What are you really eating?

When you buy a can of chopped tomatoes, that is what you expect to get—tomatoes that have been chopped up. In fact, the can might contain only 60 percent tomatoes. The rest is likely to be tomato juice plus some ingredients called food **additives**. Food additives are chemicals added to the tomatoes so they keep their color and flavor.

By law, food labels must tell you exactly what is in the package or can.

Read the labels carefully

Next time you go food shopping, check out the labels! It might be in tiny print, but you will find information about:

- the exact ingredients in the food
- where it is made or grown
- the calorie or energy content
- how it should be stored
- how many servings are in the can or pack

Knowing this helps you make a good choice. Beware! Some labels might say the contents are low-fat, but if they are high in sugar, they will still have a high calorie count.

Good fat, bad fat

We all need some fat in our diets. There are different types of fats, and some are better for you than others. Saturated fats are the bad guys. They are found in full-fat dairy products, coconut and palm oil, most fried foods, and packaged cookies. Eat less of these.

Polyunsaturated fats (Omega-3 and Omega-6 fats) are the good guys. They are found in canola, soy, and fish. Eat more of these.

Place of manufacture

Place of manufacture doesn't always mean the place where a food was grown or prepared.

Some foods are labeled *product of* or *packaged in* or both. The "product of" label tells you the name of the place where the food was grown. The "packaged in" label tells you where the food was packed.

Check where a food was grown. It is safer to eat foods that you know are grown locally or in a country with similar food standards. All foods grown in our country must comply with our safety laws. Other countries have their own safety laws, which may differ from ours.

Amount of salt

Salt is also called sodium. You only need a little of it. Products that are low in salt are preferable. Products with no salt are even better.

Artificial colorings and flavorings

Food additives include **artificial** colors and flavors that are used to make food look and taste its best. Some can cause bad reactions in certain people. To find a list of food additives, go to *http://www.cspinet.org/reports/chemcuisine.htm*

Preservatives

Most foods in packages, jars, and cans need **preservatives** to stay safe to eat. Adding preservatives makes the food last longer. It's similar to the way you add sugar to fresh fruit when you make homemade jam. Some preservatives are chemicals that people should only have in very small amounts. That's why you should eat more fresh foods than **processed foods.**

What goes into your mouth becomes part of you!

An appetite for answers

Dear Doc:

Q: My dad says there's a five-second rule if you drop food on the ground or floor. He says it takes five seconds before the food gets dirty enough to make you sick. Is he right?

A: I hate to tell you this, but your dad's completely wrong. Germs that cause illness don't hold their nose and count to five before they jump on your food! They stick to food the instant it hits the ground.

Q: Why does my aunt always want to feed me homemade soup when I have a cold?

A: When you are sick, your body burns up extra energy fighting the germs. It has to work harder if you have hurt yourself, so it can rebuild you! Your aunt loves you and is giving you extra vitamins and minerals to help you be well again. Say thanks and enjoy the soup!

Peanuts are a **legume**, not a nut. They are a good source of protein and vitamins.

Question: What's worse than finding a worm in your apple?
Answer: Finding half a worm in yor apple!

Dear Diane Dietician:

Q: All the ads for fast-food places seem to be telling me they sell nutritious foods. How can I tell what's true?

A: If you go to *http://www.nal.usda. gov/fnic/foodcomp/search/* you can look up the nutritional value of almost every food you can think of, including popular fast-food meals and snacks. It's pretty interesting reading!

Q: Should children have full-fat dairy products?

A: Dairy products (milk, yogurt, cheese) are a great source of calcium, which is important for your bones and teeth. All children need calcium each day. Until the age of two, full-fat dairy products are best. After that, it is fine to have reduced-fat dairy products. Some of them even contain more calcium than their full-fat cousins!

Q: What's so good about whole-grain foods?

A: The **fiber** in whole-grain foods takes your body longer to **digest**. This means you have more energy for longer. Also, not all the fiber is broken down. The undigested fiber helps your body get rid of waste.

> **Oranges contain folate. Your body uses folate when it makes red blood cells.**

19

Sugar!

Sugar occurs naturally in some foods, such as fruits and dairy products. Sugar is popular in the processed food industry, because it adds taste, color, bulk, and thickness to food products. It also prevents mold forming and acts as a preservative.

Sugar

Sugar is a carbohydrate and a source of instant energy. Sugar is generally made up of **glucose** (cane sugar), fructose (fruit sugar), or lactose (milk sugar). Sugar can take many forms, including white, raw, and brown sugars; honey; and corn syrup.

Refined sugar, like white sugar and superfine sugar, is a quick, simple source of energy. However, it doesn't contain other nutrients such as vitamins and minerals.

A small intake of refined sugar is an acceptable part of your diet. Experts define this as about 10 percent of the total energy (sugar) intake per day. Adding a little sugar to nutritious grain foods, such as whole-grain bread and cereals, is okay to do once in a while.

Carbohydrates and glucose

Your body breaks down carbohydrates into a simple sugar called glucose. This form of ready energy is absorbed from the small intestine into the blood, where it is delivered to every cell.

The supply of glucose needs to be constant, so the body has devised a number of systems to ensure this supply. For example, the pancreas secretes a **hormone** called insulin. Insulin regulates the amount of glucose in the blood.

Insulin allows glucose to enter body cells. It also helps with the storage of excess glucose in the liver. This supplements blood glucose levels if they start to decrease. A person with diabetes has either insufficient or inefficient insulin. This means their blood glucose levels tend to be too high.

Children with diabetes have to limit foods with lots of sugar, such as cakes and sweets. It is also important for them to maintain a healthy weight and to exercise regularly.

Recent studies suggest that there is a link between fatty, sugary foods and type 2 diabetes. This also links to being overweight. People with type 1 or type 2 diabetes should maintain a healthy weight and should limit foods with added sugar.

Sugar and being overweight

Sugar provides energy (calories), as do the other forms of carbohydrates found in breads, rice, pasta, and fruits. It's very easy to overindulge in foods with a high sugar content. Soft drinks are high in sugar. So are fruit drinks. These drinks often contain at least 12–15 teaspoons of sugar. Keep them to a minimum. While too much sugar is not the only reason for obesity, it does add to the amount of calories you consume. Eating too much of any food without doing enough exercise will cause you to become overweight.

Salt

Salt has been used in preparing food for centuries. It is used because of its taste and preservative effects.

Fat 2g
aturated Fat 0.5g
Trans Fat 0g
Cholesterol 15mg
Sodium 700mg
Total Carbohydrate 19g
ietary Fiber 1g
s 0g
Vitam
ron

How much salt should we eat?

One of the things that makes up salt is called sodium. A little sodium helps control the amount of fluids, like blood, in your body. Sodium content is listed on labels.

Adults need less than half a teaspoon of salt a day. Children need even less. We can get all the sodium we need without adding salt to what we eat.

Sodium is found naturally in many foods. It is also added to many processed foods. You might be surprised when you read the labels to find how much salt is contained in many cookies, white bread, and breakfast cereals.

Flavorings

Did you know that the "natural flavors" in your strawberry yogurt might not actually be made from strawberries? Natural flavors can be made from any plant or animal. Copies of real natural flavors are called nature-identical flavorings. Artificial flavorings might contain as many as fifty different chemicals.

Everything added to our food has to pass strict tests and laws to make sure it is safe. Some people are concerned that we don't really know how these food additives affect our health if we eat them all our lives. They worry that the chemicals might build up in our bodies and lead to health problems. How many foods with chemical additives have you eaten today?

Artificial colors and dyes

Even though all the apples in a bowl may taste the same, you will usually choose the one that looks best. You might pick one that is red all over or is a bright green. The color of food helps tempt you to try it.

For example, orange-flavored soft drinks or popsicles do not need to be orange in color. They could be clear, but people expect something that tastes like an orange to look orange. So when foods are processed, colors may be added to make them look more attractive. Most of these colorings have no nutritional value. Some can even cause bad reactions.

Artificial colors and dyes can be listed as numbers on labels. Some of these are: red number 3; blue numbers 1 and 2; and yellow number 6. Caramel, made from sugar, is the most common food coloring used.

Caffeine is found in coffee, chocolate, and soft drinks. It is mildly addictive and is a stimulant. There are even high-caffeine energy drinks, which are best to avoid.

Why eat low GI foods?

What is GI?

Some foods contain carbohydrates that are digested quickly. The energy in them is released quickly and you are soon hungry again. Other foods have carbohydrates that take longer to digest. They stay in your stomach longer, so the energy in them is released over a longer time and it takes you longer to feel hungry.

GI stands for **glycemic index**. Carbohydrate foods are given a number on a scale:

- low GI is 55 or less
- medium GI is 56–69
- high GI is 70 or above.

GI rating is decided by measuring how much the food increases someone's blood sugar levels two to three hours after it has been eaten. High GI foods increase blood sugar levels quickly, then drop down quickly. Low GI foods lead to a steadier rise and fall in blood sugar levels.

Eating low GI foods helps you have energy for longer. It also helps hold off those attacks of the hungries!

HIGH GI

128	Rice Krispies
108	donut
103	watermelon
94	pineapple
77	bananas
69	whole wheat bread
67	instant noodles
54	apple
46	skim milk
39	full-fat milk
38	whole wheat spaghetti
32	cherries
25	soybeans

LOW GI

Find a food's GI online

GI databases tell you the GI of a food. It is not as simple as saying all breads or vegetables have a certain GI. Within those foods, there are low and high GI foods. For example, lettuce has a low GI of about 10, while corn has a higher GI of about 60. Go to *http://www.lowglycemicdiet.com/gifoodlist.html* for more information.

Who will get hungry first?

Adam and Bob know they are going to play a long game of football and don't want to get hungry while they are playing. Before the game, they have a snack. Bob chooses two pieces of banana bread, while Adam has two donuts.

After about two hours, blood glucose responses to a similar quantity of a high GI food and a low GI food show that Adam's levels have dropped to where they started while Bob's are at their peak. Adam will get hungry first, because he had a high GI food. Bob will be able to play much longer, because he had a lower GI food.

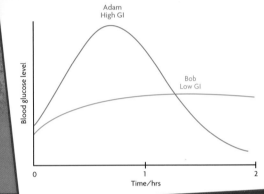

Here are some ways to stick to a low GI eating plan:

- eat breakfast cereals based on oats, barley, and bran

- eat breads with whole grains, stone-ground flour, or sourdough

- eat basmati and brown rice instead of white rice

- eat more pasta, noodles, lentils, couscous, and split peas

- eat three low GI vegetables and two pieces of low GI fruit daily

- drink plenty of water

Got the hungries?

Which of these foods will make you feel less hungry in 2 hours?

- donut
- pineapple
- bowl of noodles
- apple
- spaghetti
- whole wheat bread sandwich

The GI isn't the only important thing when selecting food. The amounts of carbohydrates, fat, fiber, and protein are all important.

Food fights

There are many food choices available to us. People have different opinions about what is best.

Raw versus cooked

A healthy diet includes both cooked and raw foods. Have you ever tried to eat a raw potato? Yuck! Cooking makes some foods (like potatoes) easier to digest.

The natural chemicals that make tomatoes red and carrots orange are needed to help protect our bodies from illness. Cooking increases their value.

Some uncooked legumes and grains contain a protein called lectin that is poisonous if we eat large amounts. Cooking destroys the lectin so the foods are safe to eat.

What about meat and chicken? Cooking can kill bacteria and the things that cause food poisoning.

Market versus supermarket

Supermarkets are a great convenience, but shopping at the local market can be a real treat. You are likely to find fruits and vegetables that you have never tried. Supermarkets sell what they think people in your area are most likely to buy. Markets sell whatever is available. You will find many interesting and delicious new flavors there. Ask the people running the stand to explain what the foods are and how to cook them.

You will often get fresher food at the market. It can cost less than at convenience stores, too. Another plus to market shopping is that you do not get packaged fruits and vegetables wrapped in plastic and on plastic trays. You can better see the quality of the food you're buying—and it's better for the environment.

Organic versus regular

Some people say that organic fruits and vegetables taste better. Other people say they can taste no difference and because organic foods are usually more expensive, they do not buy them.

Organic foods are grown and made without the use of chemicals and are farmed in environmentally friendly ways. But there is no proof that they are more nutritious than other foods.

There are very strict laws about the ways chemicals can be used on our food. Chemicals are removed when you wash fruits and vegetables and take the outside leaves off leafy vegetables like lettuce and cabbage. Organic or not is a personal choice.

School cafeterias

Who runs the cafeteria at your school? Who makes the decisions about what is for sale? Why are those foods for sale? Is it because they are good for you or because students like them? What you eat during the school day can have a big effect on how well you can concentrate and take part in activities. The government sets guidelines about what can be sold in school cafeterias.

Is your cafeteria healthy?

Check out all the items on sale in your cafeteria. Which are the healthy foods? How many items are processed? How many are freshly made when you order them? Do you get to choose what kind of bread you have? How many foods contain high levels of fat, sugar, and/or salt?

Give each food on the list a healthy-eating rating.

Rating

****	very healthy
***	healthy
**	unhealthy
*	very unhealthy

If your cafeteria sells more unhealthy than healthy food, you could make a new menu and then try to have things changed.

SOWING THE SEEDS OF A HEALTHIER LIFE

What do you get when you combine school-grown fruits and vegetables with enthusiastic students? You get an eating garden! That's what's happening at some schools in our country.

Schools with programs like this try to put students in touch with the food-growing process and encourage healthy eating habits.

Across the United States, students are learning about planting, taking care of, and harvesting fruits and vegetables.

Students, teachers, parents, volunteers, and cafeteria staff often work together in school gardens. After harvesting the fruits and vegetables they've grown, they enjoy eating them.

School gardens introduce many students to new foods as well as new ways to prepare and eat familiar fruits and vegetables.

School gardens make healthy eating fun and improve the quality and nutritional value of the students' food. Some school gardens even grow enough to supply fresh food to the school cafeteria for others in the school to enjoy!

Healthy eating hints

Here are some ideas to help make your school lunch tasty and healthy.

Pack vegetable sticks or fresh or dried fruit for snack time.

Grilled thrills: Use vegetables grilled without fat to add to your sandwich to make it taste absolutely extraordinary!

Different meals for different people: Ask friends from different cultural backgrounds to bring in foods they like from their culture for all to try.

Cookie cutter sandwiches: You can make your own healthy and nutritious sandwiches. Use whole wheat bread and fresh vegetables or meat. For a special sandwich, cut the crust off the bread and use cookie cutters to make fun shapes!

Water: It is better for you than soft drinks or fruit juices. These are expensive and have lots of hidden sugar.

Wash your lunch box: Bacteria can grow anywhere. Be sure to clean your box or bag regularly. Safety first!

Stop soggy sandwiches: If you are using moist vegetables, bag them separately, then add them to a sandwich at lunch. No more yucky, soggy bread.

Excite your lunch box tomorrow

Glossary

additives	things that are added to foods
artificial	human-made; not natural
bacteria	a tiny organism; some cause diseases
carbohydrates	energy-producing part of foods made up of carbon, hydrogen, and oxygen
digest	dissolve food in the stomach
energy	fuel for activity
fiber	rough part of foods that is not digested; helps other foods to be better digested
food-borne illness	sickness carried by spoiled food
glucose	type of sugar found in food and blood
glycemic index (GI)	rating given to foods to score how quickly they are used by the body
hormone	substance made by a body organ that is carried in the blood to another body organ that needs it
legume	plant like a pea or bean that grows its seeds in pods
minerals	natural substances like zinc and calcium found in foods
nutrients	things your body takes from food to keep you alive
nutrition	goodness of food
preservatives	chemicals added to food so it stays fresh longer
processed foods	foods that have been mixed and cooked at a factory and then put into packages for selling
protein	important part of food such as eggs, meat, and fish
vitamins	natural substances needed for good health; found in foods
wholesale	having to do with things sold in large quantities, usually for resale

For Further Information

Books

Claybourne, Anna. *Healthy Eating: Diet and Nutrition.* Portsmouth, NH: Heinemann Educational Books, Inc., 2008.

DK Publishing. *My Food Pyramid.* New York: DK Publishing, 2007.

Web Sites

Inside the Pyramid
www.mypyramid.gov/pyramid/index.html

Nutrition Explorations: Kids
www.nutritionexplorations.org/kids/main.asp

Publisher's note to educators and parents: Our editors have carefully reviewed these Web sites to ensure that they are suitable for students. Many Web sites change frequently, however, and we cannot guarantee that a site's future contents will continue to meet our high standards of quality and educational value. Be advised that students should be closely supervised whenever they access the Internet.

Index